If you were an Animal Doctor

by ELLEN LEVINE

SCHOLASTIC INC.

New York   Toronto   London   Auckland   Sydney

For Ketsel, Sneakers, Geoffrey, Tangee, and
others to come.

Special thanks to Kay Gruber for
her unflagging interest in this book and
her sharing of many cat stories;
and to Dori Brenner
for her extraordinary story
of Mr. Schwarz's cure.

With grateful acknowledgment to
Dr. Karen F. Wagner and Dr. Phillip Raclyn
of Riverside Animal Hospital;
Dr. Emil P. Dolensek, Chief Veterinarian,
and Timothy O'Sullivan,
Deputy Director of Administration of
the New York Zoological Society;
Dr. Ronald H. Bockbrader of
Tranquility Large Animal Veterinary Service;
Dr. Anita Trom of
Cranberry Highway Animal Hospital;
and Roslyn Yasser, Maggie Salvatore,
Dick Reid, and Ruth Chevion for
all their interest and help.

ISBN 0-590-41111-X

12 11 10 9 8 7 6 5 4 3   1 2 3/9

CONTENTS

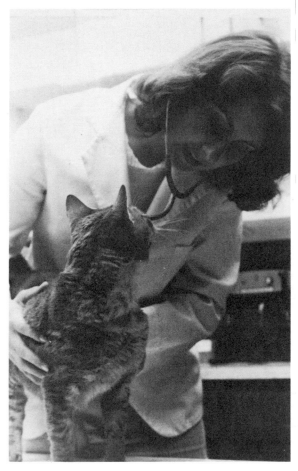

Introduction

An animal doctor is called a veterinarian, often "vet" for short. Some veterinarians work with small pets — usually cats, dogs, rabbits, and birds. Other vets work with large farm animals — cows, horses, pigs, sheep, and goats. And there are vets who work in zoos, taking care of wild animals.

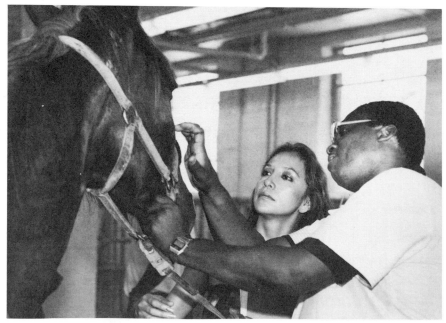

Some vets don't work with patients at all. They may inspect meat for the government to see if it is healthy before it is sold for eating. Or they may work in laboratories and do research. That is, they read, study, and think about different animal problems and try to solve them.

This book is not about all the jobs vets can do. It is about animal doctors who work with pets, large farm animals, and zoo animals.

Scientists divide all living things into the animal family and the plant family. People are in the animal family just like elephants or birds or cats. But in this book, the word *animal* means only animals that are not people.

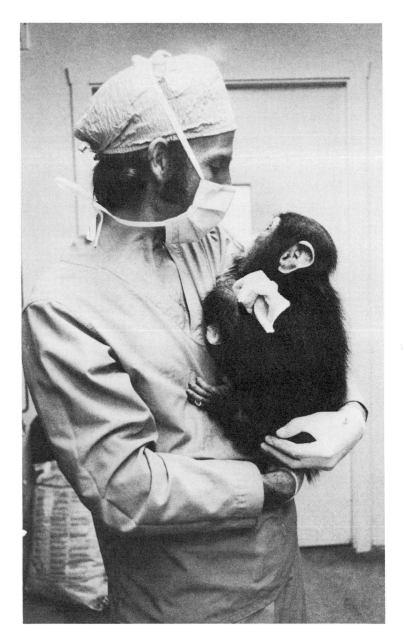

Are there special schools for animal doctors?

Yes. They are called veterinary schools, and there are fewer than 30 in the country. You must be a college graduate before you can begin the four years of veterinary school.

Your school grades must be good to get into veterinary school, and once there you will have to study very hard. You'll learn about dogs, cats, and farm animals. All other animals, including birds, are called "exotic" animals. If you study exotics, you'll learn about some zoo animals. And then if you work in a zoo, you'll do much of your learning on the job.

When you graduate from veterinary school, you will be called a Doctor of Veterinary Medicine. But learning doesn't end when you graduate. People are always discovering new ways of doing things, new medicines, and new tools.

A live cow in the classroom? It's all part of learning how to become an animal doctor.

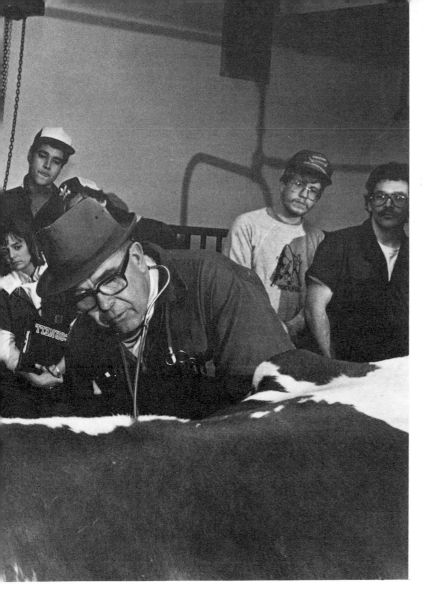

What kind of person would be a good vet?

It's important to do well in school, but you need more than good grades to be a good vet. You must like animals and care about helping them when they are sick.

You have to like to look carefully — to watch your patient's behavior to figure out what it may be feeling. And you should enjoy working out puzzles. You'll have some of the pieces: the patient's temperature, the sound of the heart and lungs, the results of blood tests, how the eyes and ears look, how the body feels, etc. Then you'll have to put all the information together to figure out what's wrong.

And you have to be interested in the whole life span of animals — you'll watch and help some being born, you'll see them as they are growing up, and you'll be there when some die. Every step is part of a whole life, and you will be part of it all.

One of the best things about being a vet is that you get to help all kinds of animals, even wild ones — like this raccoon.

What are the good and bad things about being a vet?

One of the hardest things about being a vet is that much of the time you see animals that are sick and in pain. Even though you like animals, you are the person who touches them where it hurts, sticks needles in them, or gives them medicine.

One of the best things is that you can help an animal feel better. And you can sometimes save lives. You also do see animals that are not sick. You give injections to keep them healthy. And you tell their owners about the food the animals should eat so that they don't become sick. You may spend time with frisky cats and playful dogs and soft, velvety rabbits. You may also help sheep give birth to lambs, or cure a cow who stopped being able to give milk.

If you're the doctor in a zoo, you get to see and take care of animals whose names most people don't even know. Some animals are extinct in the wild. That is, they have died out in nature. The few that are left in the whole world live in zoos. It's very important, then, to keep them healthy and strong and able to have offspring.

Small pets

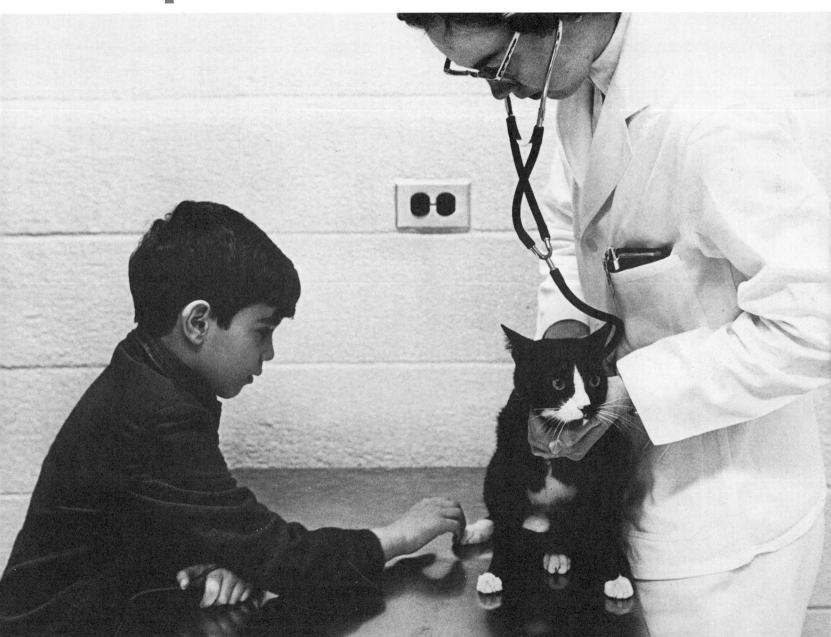

How do you know what's wrong when your patient can't talk?

Your patient can't tell you where it hurts, or whether he feels dizzy, or if she has a stomach ache. And you can't say, "Bend this way," or "Does it hurt when I do this?" So being a veterinarian is like being a detective. And there are clues and special tools to help solve the medical puzzles.

When an animal comes in for a visit, you would listen carefully to what the owner tells you about its behavior. Then you'd take the animal's temperature. You have to know what the normal temperature is, because it's different for different animals. You would look into the patient's eyes and ears with special instruments. You would feel its whole body with your hands, and then listen to its heart and lungs with a stethoscope, just like a doctor listens to the sounds in your chest.

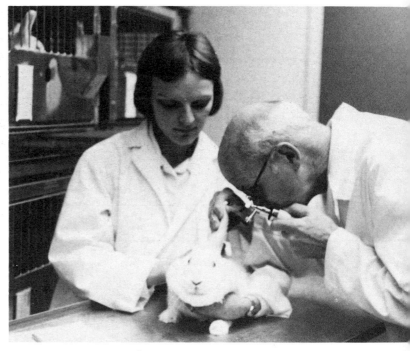

The vet uses an otoscope to examine the rabbit's ears.

Sometimes you won't be able to figure out what's wrong. And so you'll examine samples of the animal's blood, urine, and stool. Sometimes you still won't know what's wrong. You'll make a guess based on your experience, perhaps give some medicine, and wait and see.

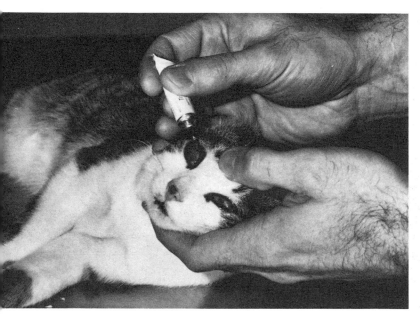

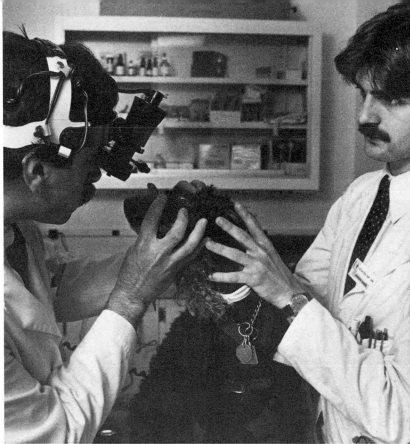

Vets have to be very careful when examining or treating eye problems.

What are the signs that an animal is sick?

Sick animals often have symptoms, or signs, like sick people. Dogs, cats, birds, and rabbits sneeze, cough, and have runny eyes and noses. Sometimes they lose hair or feathers, or pull and scratch at their skin. And sometimes they have skin rashes. Often when an animal doesn't feel well, it doesn't want to eat. It may vomit or have diarrhea or be constipated.

Sick birds usually won't sing or talk. And most animals will be depressed and mope around when they don't feel well.

What do you do when a patient is nervous?

Most animals don't like seeing the vet anymore than you like to see the doctor.

Some animals tense their bodies and stop moving when the vet starts to examine them. They are easier to examine than

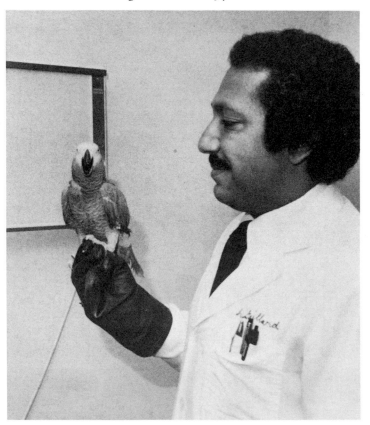

It's a good idea to wear gloves when handling some kinds of pets.

animals that start to claw or bite or wiggle or even howl. Some vets try to "jolly up" an animal before it has a chance to get too upset. They pick it up, pet it, and start talking to it in a friendly, playful voice. When this works, the animal relaxes enough to let the doctor examine it.

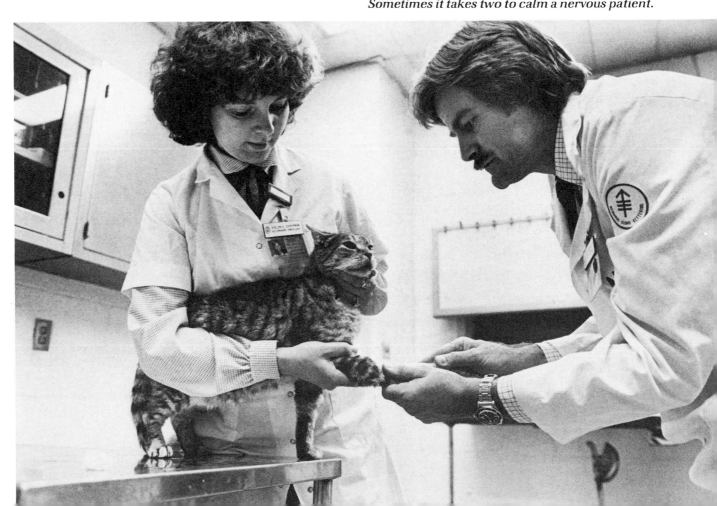

Sometimes it takes two to calm a nervous patient.

What are parasites?

Parasites, like certain worms, fleas, and mites, get their food by living on or in another creature. Some parasites are so small you can only see them through a microscope. Certain parasites live inside an animal's belly or heart, and others live in open areas like ears. Parasites are a common problem in animals.

If an animal scratches its ears a lot, it may have ear mites. These are tiny insects that live inside the ear. Or if the patient often scratches other parts of its body, it may have fleas.

If an animal has diarrhea, is vomiting, or has blood in its stool, it may have worms. A vet can use a microscope to see if an animal has certain kinds of worms. You ask the owner to bring you a stool sample, which is a piece of the droppings. Then you put the sample in a tube, add a special liquid, and lay a piece of glass over the top of the tube.

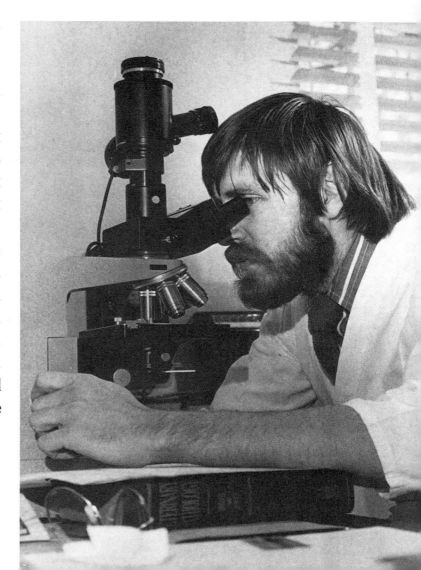

After 12 to 15 minutes, any worm eggs in the stool will rise to the top of the tube and stick to the glass. Then you put the glass under a microscope. If there are eggs, you will see them and know what kind of medicine to give the animal.

The vet can give injections, drops, special baths, salves to rub on the skin, pills — all kinds of medication to get rid of parasites.

What does "fixing" mean?

"Fixing" a dog or cat means to operate on it so that it can't have puppies or kittens. When you do this to a male, it is called *neutering*. When you operate on a female, it is called *spaying*. Sometimes the word *neutering* is used for both males and females.

Male animals that are neutered fight less, which means that they get hurt less. Also, male cats sometimes spray their urine when they are not neutered. Spaying a female cat or dog helps protect it against diseases like breast cancer or internal infections.

But there's a more important reason for spaying and neutering your pets. There are millions of cats and dogs in shelters that are killed every year because nobody adopts them. The shelters have no room to keep all of them. When you neuter pets, you reduce the numbers of unwanted newborn animals.

If you adopt a pet from an animal shelter like the ASPCA, you must promise to have it neutered.

Why is it bad for animals to be fat?

Vets often see cats and dogs that are overweight. Usually that's because the owners want to give their pets special treats. Before you know it, you have a fat pet. The extra weight puts pressure on a small animal's organs, like the heart, lungs, or kidneys. And fat puts pressure on bones and joints. Because fat animals have to drag all that weight around, most don't live as long as animals with the proper weight.

When vets take X rays of an animal, they can see all the layers of fat. That fat also makes it harder when you have to operate on a sick animal.

Once when a certain vet visited a patient at its home, he thought the owners had a hairy orange rug on the floor. It was the patient!— a very fat cat that could barely move. The vet put the cat on a diet immediately.

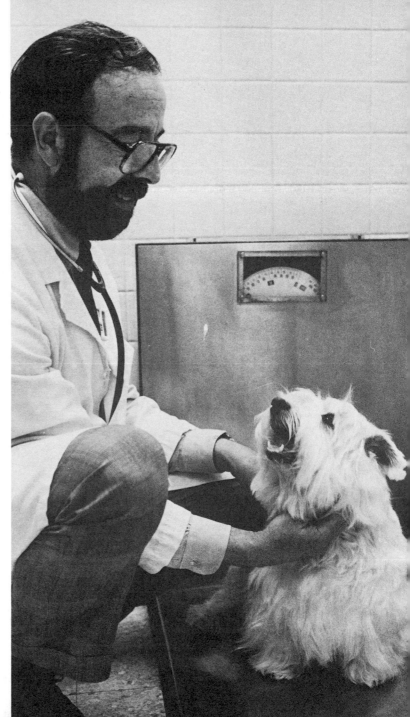

It won't be necessary to put this West Highland white terrier on a diet. She's just the right weight.

What kinds of things would you do in a day?

Many different things. You'd give yearly vaccinations; take blood samples; examine little ears, bigger ears, and large ears for mites; and tell owners about proper diets for their animals.

Then you might face a real mystery. You've examined a cat that hasn't been eating, walking, or even standing up. The tests you've done show nothing. But you know that this patient is near death. You've kept the cat overnight to see if you can figure out what's wrong.

Then you notice a lump growing at the back of the cat's head. You decide to operate. When you open up the lump, you find a large infection. And as you clean it out, you discover the cause: This cat had found a sewing needle and thread, and had swallowed both. The needle had gone through the back of the throat and up into the top of the head. The cat would have

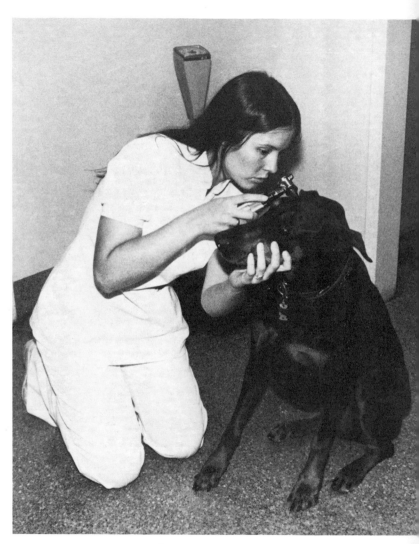

In one day, you might check a dog for ear mites...

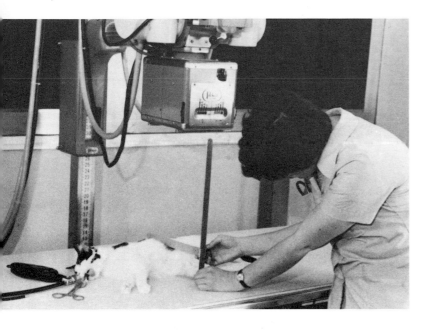

...x-ray a cat...

...and perform surgery on a patient.

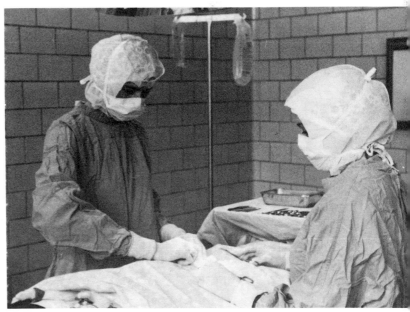

died in a day or two without the operation. Mystery solved and life saved!

Later in the day someone might rush in with a dog that had been hit by a car and had a broken leg. You'd x-ray it, set the

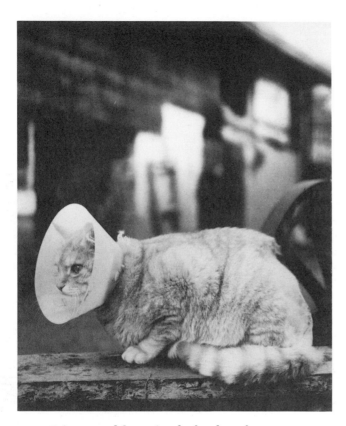

It is natural for animals that have been hurt to lick their wounds. This special collar prevents the cat from licking the wound on his back where the fur was shaved for an operation. He will wear the collar until the skin is healed.

bones, put on a splint to hold it straight, and then bandage it.

Before you go home, you might feed several animals that have no homes of their own. Some people are cruel and abandon their animals when they don't want them anymore. People who find them often bring them to you. You'd take care of these animals and try to find them good homes.

Zoo animals

Is it dangerous to work with zoo animals?

It can be. You work with poisonous snakes, elephants weighing thousands of pounds, and big cats with very sharp teeth. And so you must be careful and pay attention to what you're doing.

But there's another kind of danger — the harm *you* can do to the animals. Wild animals are not pets. They become nervous

Johnny, a 257-pound gorilla takes a deep breath as the vet listens to his heartbeat during his annual checkup. (Johnny was sedated before his physical so he isn't as dangerous as he looks.)

and upset if you handle them too often. That can make them more likely to get sick. So if you have a tiger that needs stomach surgery, when you operate, you'd also check out everything else at the same time — its teeth, eyes, and all other parts of its body. That way you cut down the number of times you have to examine it.

You also have to be careful with newborns. Sometimes when one is born, you will have to feed it. There is a danger, then, that the young one might think of you as its mother. This is called *imprinting*. To prevent imprinting, you quickly put it back with the other animals after it's finished eating. You can also try to find another young one of the same kind and feed them together. Then they pay attention to each other and not just to you. If you're not careful and imprinting happens, the animal may not be able to live with the other animals in its own group.

Zoo vets know about the dangers of working with wild animals. And rarely is a zoo vet hurt. They also work very hard not to harm the animals that are in their care.

This animal technician is careful not to let the young duiker, a small African antelope, think she's its mother.

23

How do you know what to feed the animals?

Scientists have gone to Africa, Asia, South America, and other places to study how many wild animals live. From their reports, we learn what these animals eat. Zoo vets then try to give food that will have the same vitamins and minerals in it. If the vets aren't sure what the diet should be, they make a guess based on what they know about other animals. It can take a while to figure out the right kind of food to give.

But even when scientists study animals in nature, they haven't always known exactly what to look at. Let's say you're watching a herd of African antelope nibbling on some plants. Unless you look closely, you might not see that they eat certain parts of a plant and not others. And different parts have different amounts of vitamins and minerals.

Vets who work with pets or farm animals usually don't have to feed the animals they treat. But many zoo vets do. Some work with keepers to oversee the feeding of the animals. A big zoo like the Bronx Zoo in

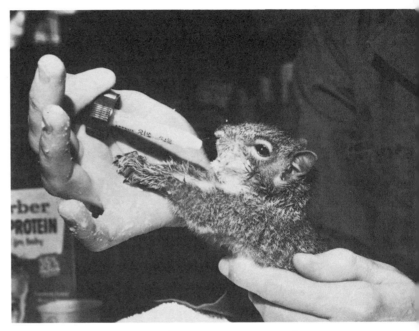

This little squirrel is being fed baby food.

New York has about 4,000 animals to feed. Every year the zoo orders 1,150 tons of hay and grains, 49,000 pounds of carrots, 122,000 pounds of fruit, 22,000 pounds of yams, 72,500 pounds of fish, and 120,000 pounds of meat. And all of it has to be prepared and fed to a hungry group of animals.

Why is finding the right food so important?

Do you know why flamingos are reddish in color? In the wild they eat a certain shellfish that has a red coloring in it. In the zoo flamingos are given different food. So zoo keepers have to add a special coloring to their food. It's like the coloring that makes carrots a reddish orange. In fact, some zoos add carrot juice to flamingos' food.

The problem of finding the right food can be very serious. One zoo vet faced a difficult problem. When he or a keeper even lightly touched Nyala antelope, some died suddenly of heart problems. He also noticed that certain wild horses were having trouble moving and turning when they

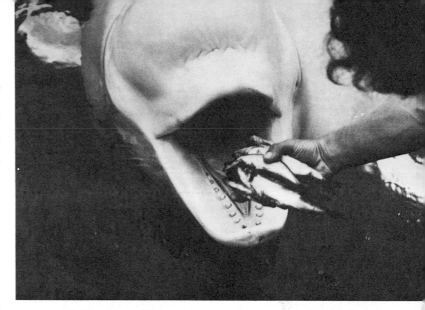

This Beluga whale eats about 40–50 pounds of fish a day.

Penguins eat fish, too — but they don't need as much.

were still young. These animals eat grasses and leafy green plants in the wild.

When the vet tested their blood and the blood of other animals who also eat grasses and green plants — elephants, giraffes, gorillas, and certain monkeys — he found they were all low in vitamin E. When these animals lived in the wild, they ate parts of plants with a lot of vitamin E. The food they ate at the zoo was low in vitamin E. So he added the vitamin to their diet and many got better. He has told other zoo vets about his research. And that's another way you learn about the right food for the animals in your care.

How do you give a wild animal an injection?

A frightened antelope, a wary jaguar, an angry gorilla, a growling lion, all feel the same way. They don't want you to come near. So how can you give them injections or take blood samples?

Zoo vets use blowguns, spears, handguns, and even bows and arrows. Instead of weapons, these become a doctor's tools. They are fitted with a needle and syringe that you shoot into an animal. The syringe is a tube that is filled with medication. Sometimes it's a medicine you want to give an animal. Other times it might be an anesthetic. This is a liquid that will put an animal to sleep for a while. Then you can examine the animal or take it to the zoo hospital for an operation.

What would you do if you had to inject an antelope that was part of a herd of very shy animals? You'd probably use a "blind." This is a hiding place, like a hut, that sits in a field where the herd grazes. You have to make sure that the animals don't see you go into the blind, or they won't come near it. One vet discovered that he could walk out onto the field with two other people and slip into the blind while the other two walked back out. The animals

An animal technician uses a blowgun to sedate the przewalski's wild horse.

27

didn't seem to realize that one person had stayed behind.

When you're hidden inside, you wait until the animal you want comes near. Then you can use your blowgun or other tool to inject it.

Are people a problem for zoo doctors?

People used to be much more of a problem than we are now. Not too long ago, you might see someone throwing food or other objects at the animals. Some people would even tease or torment the animals.

In one zoo, a healthy lion stopped eating one day. The zoo doctors x-rayed it and could see that there was something in its stomach. When they operated, they were flabbergasted to discover a beach towel inside the lion. Someone had stuck the towel in the fence around the lion area, and one of the lions had then swallowed it. That lion would have died if the vets hadn't operated in time.

Candy and hot dogs and other "people" food are not good for the animals. They

The golfers didn't mean to harm this snake. They couldn't know that the snake would mistake a ball for an egg and swallow it! Luckily, the vet was able to remove the ball, and the five-foot-long yellow rat snake survived.

have their own special diets and mustn't be fed anything else. Today many people know this. Most people respect the animals and understand that they are creatures like us. In fact, we're lucky to be able to see them at all.

What can you learn when an animal dies?

When a zoo animal dies, the vet performs a necropsy (NEE-cropsy). This means the doctor examines the animal to see what caused the death. In this way veterinarians learn a great deal about animal diseases and old age. They examine all the organs — the heart, liver, kidneys — and look carefully at the muscles, tissues, skin, and bones.

They use the information they learn to help prevent sickness in other animals.

Often zoos send skins and bones of dead animals to museums. Scientists at the museums then have materials they can study. Sometimes the bones and skins are used for exhibits, so that people visiting a museum can also learn about the animals.

Why do zoo vets have to think about the weather?

Animals in zoos come from lands all over the world. The weather in Africa or Asia, for example, is different from the weather in St. Louis; Washington, D.C.; the Bronx; or San Diego.

One winter in New York, penguin chicks from South America were treated for frostbite. The vets and keepers massaged their feet and flippers and gave them medicines. The seasons had been reversed for these animals. When it was winter in New York, it was summer where they came from. Their bodies weren't ready for the cold.

Some tapirs, which look a little like enormous pigs, had the opposite problem. In their natural home they spend the day deep in forests and come out only at night to bathe and roam around. They don't have much hair on their bodies, and zoo vets sometimes have to put suntan lotion on them so they don't get sunburned.

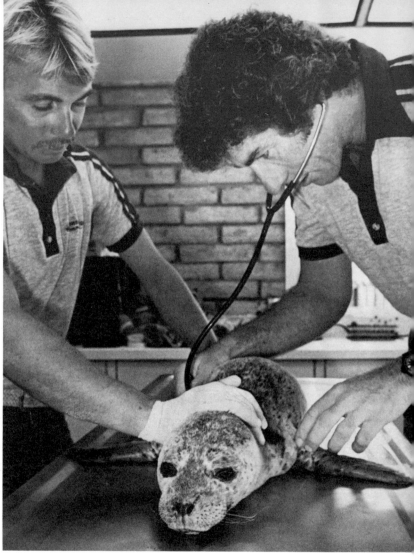

Harsh weather often affects animals. This two-month-old harbor seal is being nursed back to health after it was tossed ashore during a severe storm.

There are other problems, too. Some animals, like gorillas, are kept indoors during the winter. They come from warm climates and cannot get used to the cold in most American cities.

And so you see, vets have to know about the living habits of all zoo animals in order to keep them alive and healthy.

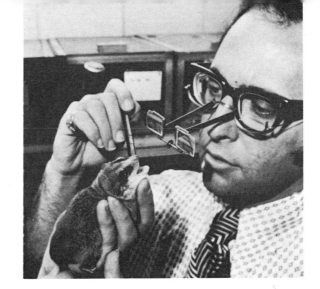

What kinds of things would you do in a day?

Zoo animals come in all sizes. Your first patient might be a tiny hummingbird that fits in half a teaspoon. Your next, a rhinoceros weighing thousands of pounds. Your office would have instruments of many different sizes.

You might examine a camel with an infection on its chest and tell the keeper what medicine to put on. Then you might check the charts the antelope keeper made to see if week-old antelope twins were gaining enough weight.

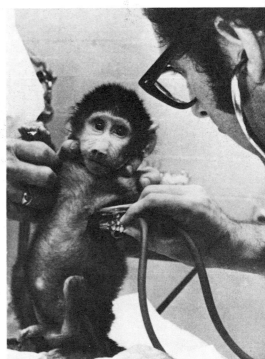

A zoo vet checks the teeth of a mouse opossum (above) and examines a young baboon (below). He lets his patients bite his stethoscope and smell it. "Like children, animals are afraid of white coats and doctor's office smells," he says.

If you had an elephant with a bad infection, you'd spend a long time giving it injections. You have to inject much more medicine into a sick elephant than you would into a sick person. But you can only give a small amount in each shot. So a sick elephant might need a total of 80 shots in one day!

At the zoo hospital, you might operate on several animals. A bird with a broken bill can't eat. So you'd have to make a plastic bill, which you would stitch and glue onto the old bill. Then you might have to saw off a hippopotamus' overgrown tooth that was eight or nine inches long, or help a porcupine mother give birth to her baby.

Parasites are a big problem in zoo animals, just as in pets, so you would regularly check the stool samples of different animals, even if they seemed healthy. That way, you'd catch a problem at the beginning.

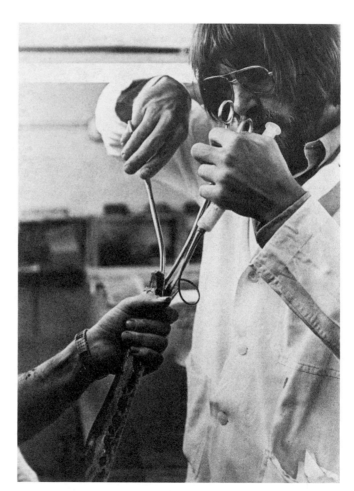

Some of the things zoo vets might do in a day: look into the throat of an Indian python...

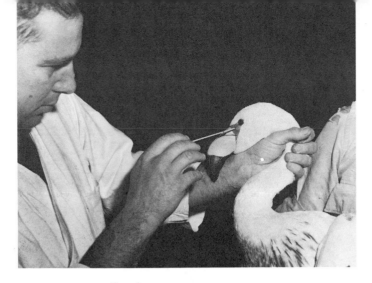

You might end your day meeting a new animal — perhaps a snow leopard — that's been shipped to you from another zoo. You'd give it an anesthetic to put it to sleep, and then you'd do a complete examination. You'd keep it at the zoo hospital until you were certain it was completely healthy. While it was settling in and getting used to its new home, you'd finally go home to yours.

...treat a flamingo...
...clean the teeth of a heavily sedated lion...

...and weigh a snow leopard.

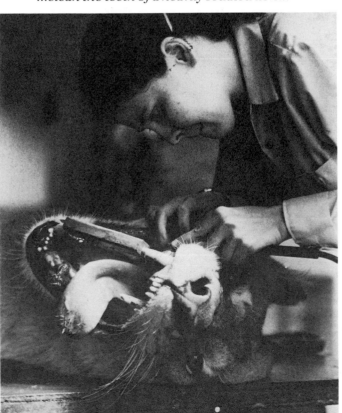

Large farm animals

Do you work in an office?

You'd probably begin and end the day in a regular office, opening your mail, answering telephone calls, reading, and doing research. But most of the time your office is the back of a truck, a field, and a barn.

Farm vets often drive trucks that are specially made for vets. In the back of the truck you'd have a refrigerator to keep certain medicines cold, a hose, hot and cold running water, electricity, a heater,

A farm vet can have two offices — one indoors, and one on wheels.

and several special compartments. In these compartments you'd bring everything you'd need when you visit a farm:

- a stethoscope to listen to sounds in the animal's body
- scalpels, which are knives for operating
- forceps, which are tools for holding things during an operation
- needles and different kinds of threads
- medicines
- rubber boots
- buckets and brushes for washing both you and the animals
- ropes, halters, and chains
- tools to take the horns off cows and goats
- pipes and tubes for giving medicine and taking blood samples
- and anything else you might need, including your lunch

You might even have a radio or telephone hookup in the truck so that farmers with emergencies can reach you while you're traveling.

The vet uses a special instrument to remove the budding horns from the dairy cow. This is often done so the dairy cows won't hurt each other with their large horns.

Do you wear special clothes when you work?

Yes. When you work with farm animals, you spend much of your time walking and working in fields and barns. Often the ground is wet and muddy. And there's manure all around.

Most important, then, are high rubber boots. Many vets wear boots that they can pull over their shoes. After they finish working at a farm, they hose down their boots to clean them.

Farm vets also wear overalls that they pull over their clothes. Sometimes you may change your overalls three times in one day. It's a good idea to change after each farm visit, so that you don't carry any mud or dirt from one farm to another. That way you protect against bringing infections or diseases from one place to the next.

You might also change your overalls several times at one farm. If you have to operate on an animal, you'd probably want

to put on fresh, clean overalls before you start.

Farm vets also have very long plastic gloves that go from their fingertips to their shoulders. You put the glove on when you examine a large animal. You have to reach inside as far as you can to feel the different parts of the animal's body. The long glove protects the animal from dirt on your hand and arm, and protects you from getting covered with manure, blood, food the animal has eaten, or other body liquids.

Who are your patients and what are their problems?

Farm vets who treat large animals have cows, sheep, goats, pigs, and horses as their patients. Most owners raise these animals in order to sell them for food, clothing, or other materials, or to show or race them. To earn a living, the owners usually must raise many animals.

And so farm vets work to keep herds, or groups, of animals healthy. Sometimes you'll see only one sick animal on a visit, but often you will examine 15, 30, 50, or even

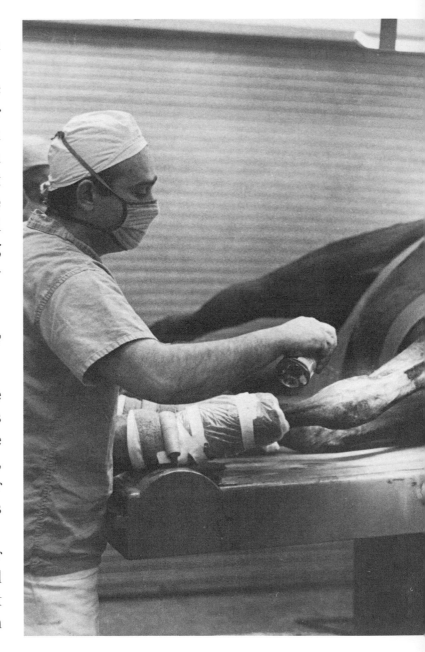

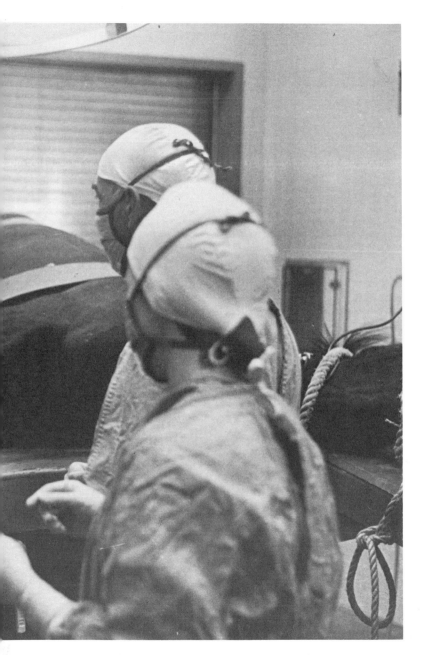

100 animals at one time. You'll see cows who can't give milk, horses with upset stomachs, sheep with problems giving birth, goats with a disease around the mouth, pigs with leg wounds or pains, and many other problems.

Sometimes vets treat mainly one kind of animal. Let's say most of your patients are dairy cows. Then one day you see a very sick horse, and you're not sure what's best to do. You'd probably refer the owner to an animal hospital that specializes in horse problems.

Special equipment is needed for large farm animals. This movable operating table weighs 3,000 pounds, large enough to support the weight of a 1,200 pound horse!

Much of your work is called "preventive medicine," because you're trying to prevent animals from getting sick. You'll give them shots so they won't lose their offspring before they're born. And you'll give a pastelike medicine or injections to kill worms and other parasites that live inside the animals.

You'll also give injections to try to keep the animals from catching certain diseases. Then you'll test the animals regularly to see that they haven't caught these diseases.

Can you get sick from working with animals?

Yes. That's why it's very important to try to prevent animals from catching certain diseases, and also to treat animals with these diseases as quickly and carefully as possible.

Cows, goats, and pigs can get sick with brucellosis (brew-sell-OH-sis), which causes them to lose their offspring before they're born. If people catch the disease, they get high fevers.

This sheep may not like the taste of the medicine, but it will help keep her healthy.

Before calves are a year old, they get vaccinated against brucellosis. There is no shot you can give to goats or pigs. When calves get their shots, they also get ear tags with numbers and ear tattoos that tell the month and year they were vaccinated. That way you know that cow number 141 got a shot against brucellosis in, let's say, March 1988.

One lung disease is very dangerous. It's called tuberculosis, or just "TB." The government in each state has laws about how often animals must be tested to see if they have TB. Usually it's every two or three years. Sometimes farm vets do the testing, and sometimes the states have their own inspectors. There are medicines for people if they catch TB. But the law in every state says that animals should be killed if they have TB because we don't want people to catch the disease from the animals.

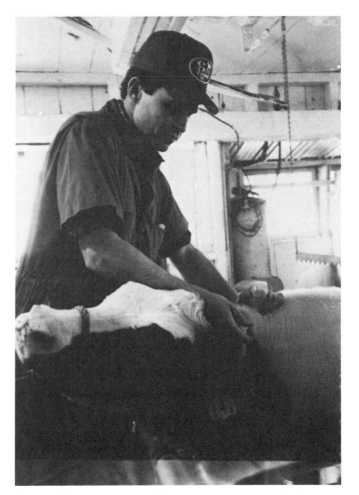

Cow # 141 is being vaccinated against brucellosis.

Pigs can have as many as 5 to 15 piglets in one litter.

Do you help with the birth of baby animals?

Sometimes. There's a special name for when each farm animal gives birth. For cows, it's called calving, sheep — lambing, goats — kidding, horses — foaling, and pigs — farrowing. Most farm animals give birth once a year, but pigs can have two litters a year. Dairy cows *must* have calves, because without calves their bodies won't make milk.

Newborns are supposed to come out headfirst. But sometimes they are turned around inside the mother. Then the vet has to put his or her arm inside the animal and turn the infant around so that it will come out properly. This happens most often with sheep, who usually give birth to two.

Sheep often have their lambs in the winter or early spring. That means you may be helping at a lambing in mud, snow, rain, or just plain cold. And an animal could start to give birth when you're fast asleep. Your phone may ring at two o'clock in the morning with a farmer's worried voice asking you to please come quickly because one of the animals is having problems giving birth.

Do you treat the mother after she's given birth?

Cows often get sick with milk fever after they give birth. Animals have something called calcium in their blood. When cows give birth, they need a lot of calcium quickly. Sometimes their bodies are so low in calcium that they can't stand up. But when you give them calcium, it works like a miracle. Within 10 minutes the cow is standing up and feeling fine.

A newborn calf is on its feet within minutes after it's born.

You can also try to prevent milk fever before it happens. About two months before the cow gives birth, you tell the farmer to give the cow food that's *low* in calcium. This may seem strange, since the cow will need a lot of calcium when it calves. But there's an interesting reason why this can work. Bones have calcium in them. And the cow can use calcium from its own bones. It takes a while for the cow's body to be able to do this, so you start the cow early. By the time it calves, the cow's body knows how to use its own calcium, and there's a good chance it won't get milk fever.

This Holstein dairy cow will soon be feeling better.

What kinds of things would you do in a day?

Your first trip in the morning might be 20 miles from your office. A farmer calls to tell you that her sheep have foot rot. Their feet have swollen, the animals are in pain, and they're having trouble walking.

Bacteria are tiny living things that you can only see through a microscope. They cause foot rot by getting into a sheep's hoof through a small cut or wound. To cure foot rot, first you trim the hooves. Then you give the sheep injections and foot baths.

Next you might visit a sick cow who isn't eating properly. When you tap the cow on its left side, you hear a *ping* sound through your stethoscope. Cows, sheep, and goats all have four stomachs. (People have only one.) When you hear that *ping*, you know what's wrong. Stomach number four is supposed to be on the cow's right side. Sometimes it gets twisted around and ends up on the left side. You have to operate to pull it back.

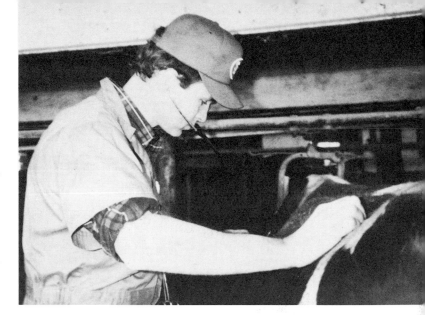

The farm vet examines the cow before her operation...

...prepares the equipment for surgery...

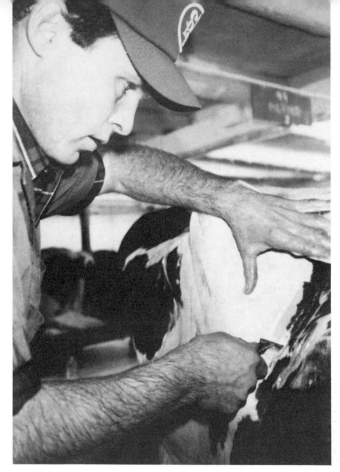

...shaves the side of the cow where the cut will be made...

You give the cow several injections so that it won't feel anything. You make a cut in its side and reach your arm in to bring the stomach back to where it belongs. Then you stitch the stomach in place and close up the side. Within a few days the cow will feel better and be able to eat properly again.

In your truck you might get a phone call about goats and pigs. The farmer describes

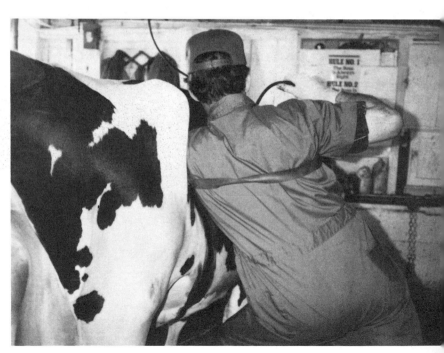

...and reaches in to put the stomach back in place.

the problem, and you decide that the goats probably have sore mouth. You know because the farmer says the skin around the mouth is dry and there are sores. The pigs might have knee infections or cuts on their legs. You drive to the farm and treat the animals.

You have to know about diseases called "lumpy jaw" or "woody tongue" or "strangles." One helpful thing is that the name tells you something about the problem. If a cow or sheep has woody tongue, its tongue becomes as stiff and hard as a piece of wood. If an animal gets lumpy jaw, its jaw bone gets infected, and there's a big lump on the side of its face. When a horse gets strangles, it coughs, has difficulty breathing, and could choke, or strangle, to death. Most importantly, of course, you have to know how to treat these problems.

Your workday usually begins early, at seven or eight o'clock in the morning. It may end at six P.M., or not until two A.M. the *next* morning, for you never know when an animal will need your help.

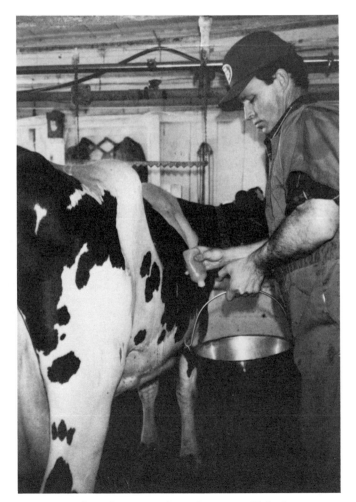

After the operation, the cow will feel better within a few days.